WHEN

THE

CHURCH

WAS

YOUNG

WHEN THE CHURCH WAS YOUNG

by

Earnest Loosley

When the Church Was Very Young

Originally Published in 1935
by
George Allen and Urwin Ltd.
Museum Street
London, England

Edited and Revised by
Christian Books Publishing House
Auburn, Maine
MCMLXXXVIII

Printed in the
United States of America

Published by
Christian Books Publishing House
Box 3368
Auburn, Maine 04210
207-783-4234

ISBN 0-940232-32-4
Library of Congress Catalog Card Number 88-63264

CONTENTS

PUBLISHER'S NOTE

It is difficult to believe that a book speaking from a viewpoint this radical appeared a generation before our time. Even today we cannot say, "The church is beginning to face these issues." She is not. But today a *few people* are beginning to. It is hoped this book will remind us that other men, in times long past, saw these foundational issues and dared to speak of them. Such a testimony from out of the past *must* enbolden *us today*, and increase the number of visionaries for *tomorrow*.

AUTHOR'S FOREWORD

The experience of the early church was very much like that of a young and growing child. There was newness and freshness in her. She knew exploration, experiment, discovery and wonder. "Some new thing" had come into the world and those who found it were engaged for years in trying to understand and to explain what it meant.

An institution is bound to grow and to become more complex, gathering about itself numerous accessories as the years pass. But that development must be in harmony with the original spirit and intention of the movement, and not restrain or divert or enfeeble it. The days of the first warm enthusiasm, of the first vivid inspiration, and of original contact with creative personality must ever be kept; and the ideals then imparted must fashion the whole course of outward development. The essentials are the things that are present at the beginning.

It will scarcely be denied that many unessential things have crept into the church's life, and that a disproportionate share of its energy is absorbed by these unessentials. Indeed, in the opinion of Dr. C. E. Raven, something even more serious than this had happened.

> "A profound alteration has taken place in the character of the religion of Jesus. This difference is not merely one of externals nor is it inherent in the necessity of growing older. The evidence demonstrates that fundamental changes have taken place in the inner life of the church, in its relationship to Christ and to God."

It should be a salutary experience to remind ourselves that things were not always the way they are now. The church, with more or less conscious aim, has made itself what we now know it to be. But when it was very young, it carried a minimum of paraphernalia, and did its work the more effectively because it travelled light.

We may yet find that the way of wisdom for ourselves lies in the pursuit of a similar policy.

What traditions have been introduced for expediency may now be left behind, also for reasons of expediency. The Spirit is still alive, and is willing to lead the church to new ventures of faith and practice. Hear the closing paragraph of Dr. Streeter's book, *The Primitive Church.*

"It is permissible to hint that the first Christians achieved what they did because the spirit with which they were inspired was one favorable to *experiment.* Perhaps the line of advance for the church today is not to imitate the forms but to recapture the spirit of the Primitive Church."

The Author

PART I

When the Church Was Young

It Had:

    No Buildings

    No Denominations

    No Fixed Organizations

    No New Testament

    No Vocabulary of Its Own

    No Dogmatic System

    No Sabbath Rest (in the Gentile World)

1

NO BUILDINGS

When the church was very young, *it had no buildings*. Let us begin with that striking fact.

That the church had no buildings is the most noticeable of the points of difference between the church of the early days and the church of today. In the minds of most people today, *"church"* means first a building, probably something else second; but seldom does "the church" stand for anything other than a building. Yet here is the fact with which we start: the early church possessed no buildings and carried on its work for a great many years without erecting any. This fact has something significant to teach us concerning the character of the church.

In the first few years of her history it was the

temple which was the center of the church's meetings. The authorities soon turned against the church and denied the use of the sacred spot for the preaching of the gospel.

Similarly, when the movement spread beyond Palestine, it was generally in the Jewish synagogue that the apostles *began* their mission (Acts 13:5, 14, 43; 14:1; 17:1, 2, 10, 17; 18:4, 26; 19:8). Nothing could have been more opportune, more providential, than the opening afforded by these select Jewish communities wherever the apostles went.

But when these doors were closed to them, as they soon were (18:7; 19:9), what followed? The apostles had no thought of acquiring or erecting "Christian" buildings. There is no sign of the existence of any Christian building during New Testament times or for long after. [1] There was practically nothing in the way of church building until the third century, and nothing with any pretension to architecture until after the conversion

---

1. The reference to a synague in Jas. 2:2 is not an exception. It should almost certainly be understood in the sense of "gathering" or "meeting." See Mayor's *James*, 3rd Edition, p. 82f.

of Constantine early in the fourth century. [2] During all this time the church carried on her mission without buildings of her own, without property, and without the burdens and responsibilities that the holding of property implies.

There was wisdom in this self-denial. The expectation of the Lord's early return would naturally cause any outlay on property to appear unnecessary. This consideration ended before many decades passed; yet even after the expectation of His immediate return subsided, *still* the church had no buildings.

What *did* continue were fresh outbreaks of persecution which occurred during the first three centuries of the church's history. In the course of such experiences, the property of the church, if it had possessed any, would have been the first thing seized. Property and buildings would have been even more vulnerable than Christians themselves to be attacked and confiscated. [3] There was wisdom, therefore, in the Christians' policy of refraining from building places of worship.

2. *Encyclopaedia of Religion and Ethics, I: 340, 697; III: 247.*
3. E.g. the Edict of Valerian, A.D. 257, confiscating the Christian churches and cemeteries.

Where, then, did the Christians meet for worship and for fellowship? There is evidence that in some places Christians protected their legal position by registering themselves as burial societies, [4] and as such they rented *scholae*, or public rooms, which served as places of meeting. (These developments, however, belong to a later time.)

In the apostolic age, Christians were accustomed to meet in private houses.

For this there is abundant evidence in the New Testament. The reference to the temple (Acts 2:46) has its immediate sequel in their "breaking bread at home." This is repeated at the end of Acts 5: "And every day, in the temple and at home, they ceased not to teach and to preach Jesus as the Christ." Not all the members' homes would be equally convenient, but those who had the accommodations appear to have placed them willingly at the disposal of the church. The life and fellowship of the community became closely associated with the homes of its members. Among the first to open the doors of her house to the Christians was Mary of Jerusalem, the mother of John Mark. When Peter was delivered from prison in the middle of the night, it was to this

4. T.R. Glover, *Jesus in the Experience of Men*, p. 157.

house that he instinctively made his way, and there "many were gathered together and were praying" (12:12). Elsewhere we read in the New Testament of Aquila and Priscilla having "the church in their house" (Rom. 16:5; I Cor. 16:19), and also Nymphas (Col. 4:15), and Philemon (v. 2).

In Corinth, after leaving the synagogue, Paul carried on the work in the house of Titus Justus, "one that worshipped God, whose house joined hard to the synagogue" (Acts 18:7).

These references indicate a widespread and general practice of meetings being in houses! We are forced to see the early Christians as regularly meeting together in small, homely groups, conducting their worship, enjoying their fellowship, and celebrating their communions, amid the familiar surroundings of their living rooms!

Sometimes, for purposes of evangelizing, the apostles would launch out and hire a building. At Ephesus, (after the breach with the synagogue authorities) Paul "reasoned daily in the school of Tyrannus" (19:9). Apparently this was a lecture hall *that might be hired or loaned for such a purpose.*

It never seems to have occurred to Paul to

start a building fund anywhere in order to provide the local church with a place of worship. The fund he did start had an altogether *different* purpose: the assistance of the poverty-stricken Christians in Jerusalem (Rom. 15:25-27; I Cor. 16:1-3; II Cor. 8:1-4; 9:1-2; Gal. 2:10; Acts 24:17). The support of those who were entirely set apart for the work also became a recognized point of giving in the Christian communities (I Cor. 9; I Thess. 2:9; II Thess. 3:8, 9).

Yes, they collected money. But *today* a building comes first, community second. Philanthropy today comes in a long way behind as the third claimant. Philanthropy, when the church was young, seems to have come *first*, the support of workers *second*, while the cost of buildings was represented only by the occasional hiring of a hall.

The early Christians knew nothing about special efforts for the purchase of a site, the erection of a church building, or paying off a debt for one. Energies *not* required for building were available for uses of a more spiritual nature.

Today our property is often our problem. In trying to evangelize a neighborhood, we erect a building and become *rooted* to that particular

8

spot. The neighborhood, in the course of a generation or two, may change completely; but there we are, stuck with our building. The area may give place to shops, offices and warehouse; but the structure remains, immovable and imperishable.

To follow a population, and to minister to its spiritual needs, becomes much more difficult when the problem is presented as one involving a site and a building.

To the early Christians the problem did not present itself. It is almost impossible for us to think ourselves back into a stage of development before that of church buildings. To us, the whole life and work of the church have been centered for hundreds of years in buildings.

But *are* we right? Evangelization of people and the building of a building are one and the same. *Must* we secure a site and build a church building in order to reach and win men for Christ? The communists have not regarded such steps as prime necessities for the spread of their propaganda. They do not seem to think that, in order to win the world for communism, the great thing to do is to build halls and fill them with audiences.

The purpose to which we are devoting our efforts is not to fill buildings, but to win men to a new way of life, with Christ as Savior and Lord. The witness to the new way of life must be born primarily in the ordinary, day-to-day course of life.

During this century the population has become far more mobile. The home need not be placed in the downtown center of population in order to secure the amenities of life. Consequently the tendency is for houses to spread widely over the countryside. A village used to be a collection of houses clustering round a church. Nowadays, the population may be everywhere. [5]

This "ribbon development" adds greatly to the church's difficulty in following the population. Where are the church buildings to be put, when there is no obvious center of communal life? They cannot be planted at intervals of a mile or two all along the highway; but nothing less than this would solve the problem, at least from the point of view that we have been accustomed to think. Moreover, nearly every house has a radio providing all

5. Little could this author imagine suburban sprawl, condos, shopping centers, high rises and second homes!

the preaching one could hope to hear. [6] The element left unprovided for is the sense of fellowship with others in worship and praise and prayer. A sense of community *and* meeting in homes are two almost inseparable elements.

Here is a pertinent question. How would the church have met the present and ever changing situations today, had it never built church buildings? Is not the answer this: she would have developed and extended the idea of "house-churches," encouraging groups of neighbors to meet in one another's homes, to share in group fellowship.

A large part of the problems confronting us today cannot be solved within our traditional practice of erecting places of worship. We must set ourselves to thinking along other lines. And the first century church may have some useful ideas to suggest, simply because they had not yet subscribed to the doctrine that if you want to win a man for Christ, the main thing is to get him to sit down in a church building during a service.

6. If he could see us now! Armed with our 300-channel T.V. dish, our six color T.V. sets and four video players, our 200 audio tapes, over 10,000 music tapes and our ultra *stereophonic* electronic multiphased modality, duel axulated stereo set.

But there is a deeper question still, underlying this subject of the relation of buildings to the spread of Christianity. Because the church possessed no buildings, it was in less danger of elevating the material at the expense of the spiritual. We are in danger of attaching an exaggerated importance to buildings and "things" that go with them.

Listen to your Lord: The hour cometh, when neither in this mountain, nor in Jerusalem, shall ye worship the Father ... The hour cometh, and now is, when the true worshippers shall worship the Father in spirit and truth. For such ones doth the Father seek to be His worshippers. God is spirit: and they who worship Him must worship Him in spirit and truth" (John 4:19-24)

In those words Christ enunciated the fundamental concept of worship. "Place is irrelevant: 'here' or 'there' matters nothing. It is not the outer habitation that you need, but the life, the spirit within. Do not be preoccupied with questions affecting only the material and the outward: concentrate upon the spiritual and the eternal."

The most solid of all material things is still subject to decay. Moth and rust have their way.

Church buildings are constantly falling into decay in precisely the same way as secular buildings.

"These things are thus all to be dissolved" (II Pet. 3:11).

Jesus also said "Seest thou these great buildings? There shall not be left here one stone upon another which shall not be thrown down" (Mark 13:1 f.) Tennyson wrote of the city "built to music, therefore never built at all, and therefore built forever." [7] Not perishing stone, but immortal human lives endure. *Our supreme concern must be with the things that will last when the most substantial of earthly things shall have perished.* The chapel in which you worship may someday be demolished. What then? The real, abiding church is not built of brick or stone. The real church and her architecture conform to none of the patterns given in the guidebooks. She is built up from human material which the Lord fashions day by day into a closer resemblance to His divine ideal. Worship is not a matter of stated hours and special days and consecrated places. Worship consists of the opening of the mind and heart towards worshiping God. Such building is

7. *Gareth and Lynette.*

one which *the true servants* of Christ have been building from earliest days.

When the church was very young, she had no buildings except the one not built with hands.

2

NO DENOMINATIONS

When the church was very young, it had no denominations.

Here is another big difference as compared with the the church of today. We associate the Christian church with denominations, almost as a matter of course. We commonly use the word "church" in a sense in which it is never used in the New Testament. "Which 'church' do you belong to?" But in the New Testament "the church" means either the whole body of believers in Christ or a local congregation in a specific city. "Church" never denoted any section divided from the rest in belief or practice.

In spite of difficulties that threatened to make a grievous breach in the fellowship, this still represented the ideal of the church at the end of her first century of existence.

In describing the earliest days of the church, Luke frequently uses the expression "with one accord" (Acts 1:14; 2:46; 4:24; 5:12; 15:25). The unanimity of the followers of Christ is a characteristic Luke felt was important to note. And the leaders honestly strove to keep this reality, though in practice it is one of the most difficult of all things to maintain.

Indeed, it was not very long before conflicting schools of thought arose within the circle of the church's life and organization. The well-known hymn "Happy the Souls That First Believed," describes the situation as Charles Wesley conceived it:

"Meek, simple followers of the Lamb,
They lived and spake and thought the same."

If ever that was true, it did not remain true! If the early church knew nothing of the denominational divisions that marked its later history, it was not because there was one flat level of uniformity in thought and practice, but because something bound them all together in unity, in spite of variations in point of view. And workers fought *for* unity while today men fight to keep division.

A difference of opinion arose in those early days that was important enough to match any doctrinal dispute we have ever faced in our day. The contrast between their day and ours was in the stature of the men involved.

The Council of Jerusalem described in Acts 15 is of great historic importance, and full of significance. One can see that this was a situation out of which denominational divisions could very easily have arisen. The danger was realized by the leaders of the church, and steps were taken to stop the division. If the decisions arrived at (v. 28 f.) seem to us to lack something of logical consistency, at any rate they preserved the unity of the church.

Throughout the history of the church, similar opposing tendencies can be traced—the broad and the narrow, the liberal and the conservative, the tolerant and the strict, and only too often the temper and the spirit of the rival leaders have been such that compromise was ruled out and a *modus vivendi* was neither sought nor found.

The church in Corinth reveals another influence at work that tended towards division.

Certain sections of the membership emphasized their respective loyalties by such party cries as "I am of Paul, and I of Apollos, and I of Cephas"; while some (perhaps in the spirit of "A plague on both your parties") declared themselves to be "of Christ" (I Cor. 1:12). Use of personal names as a rallying point for factions is a phenomenon that is often witnessed in religion: Lutheran, Brownites, Wesleyan, Campbellites, etc. How easily a separatist movement in the church may center around the name of some outstanding leader.

It is to the credit of the early church that, in spite of acute disagreements that sometimes arose (e.g. Gal. 2:11), the personal relations of the leaders were a *unifying* rather than a *divisive* influence.

Yet another possibility of division arose in connection with *organization*. As the work extended and numbers multiplied, on what lines were the arrangements for the common life of the church to be planned? Would it function more effectively and congenially in this way or in that?

In the *earliest* days, practically all who came within the fellowship of the community of the body of Christ had previously experienced "going to the synagogue." At a later stage, when converts were added directly from the Gentile world, the Gentiles brought with them no previous acquaintance with the synagogue. But they were not lacking in experience with Christ nor in the experience of fellowship with one another.

With so many precedents and models surrounding them (provided by synagogue, society, family and government) how was the church to organize its common life? Something could be said for each of the influences around them. There was no valid reason why each separate Christian community should adopt exactly the same model.

Dr. Streeter (*The Primitive Church*) holds that there are traces of several distinct expressions of the church in the New Testament and in early Christian literature. Episcopalian, Presbyterian and Independent can all justify their particular church order by reference to the Scripture.

It is clear that there was abundant room for division whenever discussions as to "order" arose. If anyone were foolish enough to put forward the idea that one type was right and all the others wrong, such a contention would prove to be an anvil on which the church might split.

Here, again, was an element that might easily have produced "denominations." But it did not!

The early church did not preserve its unity because of the absence of possible ground of division. The possibilities of separation were there!

Was denominationalism—as it exists today—inevitable? Is the only alternative a flat uniformity? If diversity can only be enjoyed on the basis of separation, then we must accept separation. At any cost, we must have the freedom to think for ourselves, to advocate our own point of view, to make an individual contribution to the faith to which we belong. If this liberty can only be enjoyed in a system of separate communities, then we must accept the situation.

But somehow the church, when it was very young, succeeded in maintaining its unity in spite of the fact that so many divisive tendencies were already at work.

How did she keep the unity of the spirit in the bond of peace? In spite of divergence of thought, personal differences of leaders, varieties of expressions and authority, and other factors that wrought division before many years had passed, how did she keep unity?

Fortunately we have documents that show us how one or two of the leaders actually faced and dealt with the problem.

Corinth was perhaps the place, of all others, in which the elements of divergence manifested themselves. It was what any modern minister might describe as "a very difficult church."

"The Corinthian Church was full of quarrelling—not merely about belief and practice, but about more concrete things, which the members took to the law courts; and there were worse scandals still. The Greeks, who formed the majority, had all the defects of the Greek mind, but little, it would seem, of its grandeur; and the Church bristled with every kind of wrong-headedness. Its members came from Judaism and heathenism. There were ascetics and vegetarians ... there was a "Spirit" party, subject to trances and visions and ecstatic speech with 'tongues.' Allied with this party, or perhaps at variance with it but certainly akin to it, were the antinomians—set free from the body, living in the spirit, and therefore free to let the body have its pleasures while the soul rose superior to them. Theosophy of one kind and another flourished, and every other kind of crotchet—baptism for the dead being one of them—in an atmosphere of sloppy thinking." [8]

Here were all the elements of party spirit and denominationalism run mad.

What was Paul's method of dealing with a threatening danger of this kind, so likely to split the church into numerous quarrelling sects?

The point of vital and lasting importance is reached when Paul passes from particular details and fastens attention upon *ideals* and *principles*. He introduces the concept of the church as the body of Christ and proceeds to unfold and develop all that this means (I Cor. 12).

"You are a very mixed company of people, very different from one another in all kinds of ways; as different as the members of the human body are, in size and shape and position and function. But you are not antagonistic the one to the other, any more than the members of the body are mutually antagonistic. You are not independent of one another, any more than the members of the body can

8. *Jesus in the Experience of Men,* p. 155f.

pretend to be independent. You dare not be unruly or wrongheaded in your behavior, any more than a single member or a group of members of the body dare be rebellious or disloyal to the whole. You are all in fellowship with one another. The rich variety of your gifts enhances the usefulness of the organism as a whole. You have a fine range of powers which you can employ in mutually helpful service. All of you, with all the variety of your endowments, may share in and contribute to the one life of the body as a whole; for the body is not this or that member, this or that group, this or that section; but all of you, closely knit together.''

Paul's parable is a piece of inspired statesmanship. In his working out of the idea we have one of his masterpieces. The body suffers today—suffers needlessly—because Paul's message is unheeded. His lesson in unlearned today.

But there is more to follow.

"And still I have to show you a more excellent way,'' says the apostle. "What you really need, all of you, is more love. Don't be quarrelsome and unkind and self-assertive: love one another. Don't be touchy and uncharitable, short-tempered and ready to believe evil: love one another. Love is patient and kind. Love knows no jealousy. Love makes no parade; gives itself no airs. Love is not unmannerly, nor selfish, nor irritable, nor mindful of wrongs. Love does not rejoice in injustice, but joyfully sides with the truth. Love can overlook faults. Love is full of trust, full of hope, full of endurance. Love never fails." [9]

Such teaching goes to the very root of the matter! Would not that have prevented nearly all the separations that have taken place throughout the history of the church? Would not that heal nearly all the divisions that exist today? Would it not show that we are indeed His, whose name we bear?

When the church was very young, there were no denominations. When the church grew up, the ideal of unity was lost sight of. That was *not* an asset! The church must seek after that unity again today. And when the church militant shall have become the church triumphant, its divisions will disappear along with all other imperfections.

Names and sects and parties fall:
Thou, O Christ, art all in all.

9. I Cor. 13 Weymouth and Moffatt.

24

3

NO FIXED ORGANIZATION

When the church was very young, it had no fixed organization, and no body of rules.

To grasp the full significance of this needs some reflection. Today there is no institution in the world that is more highly organized than the Christian church! As for rules, there is *at least* one for *every* situation. And the total collection of these rulers forms a *corpus* of large dimensions. My own section of the church contains eight hundred pages of policy. Whenever I want to know what is the right thing to do in a certain situation, I consult an elaborate index. It saves a lot of trouble to "live by rule." Our rules settle it, and there is no appeal.

A church *without* organization—such a thing is almost unimaginable! Yet Jesus launched His church in this condition. And He expected it to be able to function without the impediment of organization. Nor had He spent His time upon earth in telling His followers how the movement was to be organized and regulated. He had something far more important to do. [10] As he had once sent them forth "without purse, and wallet, and shoes," so now He sent them forth again without the equipment that the church today finds so necessary to its work. Yet the apostles confessed that they "lacked nothing" (Luke 22:35). Let us admit that the vast organization we have belongs to the category of the unessential, and that without it there could still be a Christian church, effective and victorious!

A church expression which is the expression of life, and which modifies and adapts itself to changing conditions, is one thing. A form that is fixed and rigid is another thing.

The form and organization of the Christian church are not to be reckoned among its primary and essential features. Such things are demonstrably unessential and secondary.

"For the first hundred years or so all church organization must have been

10. A.C. Benson, *The House of Quiet*, chap. xx.

more or less informal, and a matter of moral prestige rather than of legal right." [11]

The early Christian documents show a development which was not absolutely uniform nor identical in every place. Development was marked by local differences and modifications. This again is exactly what we might expect, if we believe that life fashions form and not that form produces life. They disposed of the idea that *one* form is essential or unalterable.

From the first chapter of Acts onwards, we see arrangements being made for the united worship of the community. "With one accord" they "continued steadfastly in prayer" (v. 14). The next chapter (v. 46) indicates some development following upon the events of the Day of Pentecost. "Day by day, continuing steadfastly with one accord in the temple, and breaking bread at home," they nourished and sustained their new-found experience by means of worship and fellowship. Their common life is carried a stage further in the fourth chapter (v. 32 ff.). Not content with a spiritual expression of fellowship which pervades their circle, they extend that spiritual expression to material things, and agree to a common sharing of

11. Streeter, *The Primitive Church*, p. 258.

27

possessions. So far as one can judge, this new step was regarded at the time as being just as much a part of the church as earlier functions. If anything belonging to those early days had a right to be regarded as a precedent for the future, this practice had as clear a claim as any. Why do we study so closely other activities of that era, but not his one. This "experiment" was allowed to lapse. Nevertheless, it is interesting to enquire why this or that selected expression of the life and fellowship of the early church should be regarded as a precedent valid and binding for all time. How is it, on the other hand, that the elasticitity and informality of the early church was allowed to lapse out of existence without a qualm?

From year to year the expression of the church changed in order to express its inward life. "Form" was the creation of the spirit. That "form" was flexible, not rigid; adaptable, not final. Each step is taken with the assurance that the living Spirit is present to suggest and to guide.

When the presence and guidance of the Spirit can no longer be counted upon, it will not matter whether the organization is flexible or rigid! In either case the church will have ceased to fulfil its function in the world.

Any group which comes together for a definite purpose contains men with a variety of gifts. Common sense says that we should use each man's gifts in the way that will best contribute to the realization of the goal. That seems to have been the underlying idea of the early Christian community.

The church did not spring from the mind of Christ with its orders and ranks and hierarchies completely planned. The field was clear for such steps and arrangements as might commend themselves to the church in the course of her development. The gifts and character of Stephen, Philip, and the rest of the seven were employed in a way that matched men to opportunity and gifts to need.

It was the presence of the men with their gifts that led to the creation of the office, not vice versa! Living men in contact with their Master in the context of a new movement were also now eager to further the work in any way open to them. According to each man's ability, work was given him to do. According to the direction in which he appeared to show promise, a man was trained for the work of preaching, teaching, presiding, collecting, or whatever service could be rendered by him to the church.

Offices multiplied because there were men endowed with a wide variety of gifts.

The gifted one must always come first. Not the office first; the *man* first! An office filled by one not gifted to that office is a useless piece of machinery. The inner life and the experience of the church must express itself and clothe itself in recognizable forms. But the forms may legitimately posses a wide range of variety, if so be that they truthfully express the inward spirit. The realm of organization is one in which no one has a right to claim universal identity. No division, no schism, should ever be based upon mere questions of organization or order or form. There is scope for wide difference among those who share in the one essential Christian experience. And when the church was very young it had no organization and no regulations.

4

NO NEW TESTAMENT

When the church was very young it had no New Testament. *The church is older than the New Testament.*

The movement in Palestine, described in the gospels and the early chapters of Acts, was a movement *without* the aid of literature! In this respect it is strikingly unlike modern religious movements. Jesus wrote no tracts, no sermons, no autobiography, no journal, no apologia. When He departed, He left no literary remains and appointed no literary executor.

The first impulse of the disciples was not an impulse to write, but to preach.

When the twelve and the seventy were sent forth, they were given a commission to preach.

The word used in the last great commission of Matt. 28 is "teach." The spoken message is clearly what He referred to. The apostles were not men with literary training. The atmosphere in which they labored was not literary.

The literature arose out of the situation. As the church developed, men wrote to speak to needs, needs dealing specifically with the church! Neither the gospels nor the epistles can be really understood apart from the actual circumstances of the church's development. Simply to sit in the study and compare and analyze and dissect the documents is a very imperfect method of reaching an understanding of the New Testament or the church when it was young. The church, and her literature, are the product of a great surging spiritual move. She must be understood in relation to that movement.

Let us try to picture the church of the earliest days, noting the frequency of Christ's own word "witness." (e.g. Luke 24:48), [12] (We may understand this word to mean "to propagate.") How did the apostles begin to fulfill their task to witness? In Peter's first public address he arraigned his hearers before the bar of their own

12. Acts 1:8,22; 2:32; 3:15; 4:33; 5:32; 10:39,41; 13:31.

consciences, showing them what a deplorable mistake they had made in crucifying Jesus.

In this first address there is a literary element which takes the form of three quotations from already existing literature—the Old Testament. The reason for these quotes, of course, is that the first audiences these men addressed were Jewish. On most points, therefore, there was agreement between preachers and hearers, and a great deal could be taken for granted. Their words were mainly directed towards establishing that Jesus was (in spite of His crucifixion) the Messiah.

As converts were won to the movement, the need of giving them further instruction and training became urgent. The new ones needed to be brought up to date so as to be in the same position as those who had actually heard the words of Jesus. Some account of His life had to be compiled. Manifestly, the men who knew these things were those who must tell them. But remember that the *earliest* days were pre-literary! Everything was oral.

Please note that as late as the book of Acts, the man Theophilus was reminded that everything he was taught was "by word of mouth" (Luke 1).

All of past Jewish life, practice, and culture were built on the *oral* concept of passing on information—not literature! Word of mouth! Oral instruction, by repetition, was the schoolmaster's way of teaching. Such Jewish literature was never written down until *after* the beginning of the Christian era. Before that, their sayings were *memorized* by the disciples of Jewish teachers.

Nor can we say of the early believers that there was one uniform "course of study" which was in use everywhere. Not until the printing press was there identity of presentation. Each church would have its own approach. Moreover, each apostle had his own way of telling *the* story, and each man tended to emphasize those parts of that story which especially appealed to him, or that part which burned in him because of what it had done to him spiritually.

When the church was very young, the story was told and retold countless times, to all kinds of audiences, critical and sympathetic, outside the church and inside. All of this and no written literature!

But that was the church in Palestine and Syria. As soon as the era of expansion began, the resources of the church became subject to increasing strain. The demand for qualified exponents could not be met everywhere by first-hand witnesses of the events of the Lord's life. This situation was one ingredient that caused the message to be put in written form. This situation made the written word inevitable. (This situation probably produced the first written attempt at a gospel.)

Now the landmarks become more familiar. In fact it is not necessary to trace the story beyond this point. By 65 A.D. most of the New Testament epistles had also been written, springing (as the gospels did) out of the actual situation developed in the churches and among the workers! Not for many years would it be true to say, in the fullest sense, that the church had its New Testament. (The process of final selection was not complete until the fourth or fifth century.)

Most first century believers never saw and were never concerned about a "New Testament"! Do you realize what this meant? It was possible for the church to exist and to be really effective without the New Testament! It was the revelation of God in Jesus Christ and the interpretation of that story that came to men from the lips and pens of those who were first commissioned to tell it that turned an empire upside down! The New Testament is a product of the life of the early church when it was in closest touch with the actual disciples of Jesus. The church was surging with the new spiritual experience that sprang from personal contact with the Master. That is its supreme value! Knowing *Him* accounts for its unchallenged authority. Knowing *Him* embodies the meaning of the new life in Christ. The ones who delivered the message *knew* Him.

There was an overruling providence of God in the giving of the gospels to the world, we may be quite certain. In such a supremely important matter as the record for future generations of the revelation given in Christ, the hand of God was unquestionably at work. But it was also God's hand that caused a church to come alive and grow, multiply and shake two continents . . . *without* a New Testament!

If the apostles had met in council at Jerusalem to decide as to the writing of a record of Christ's life . . . one which would serve for people living two thousand years hence, what would they have made of it? Certainly something very different from what we have now. Different, *but not better.*

They could not have composed anything so representative, so adequate, so entirely worthy. By writing to meet their own immediate needs, to supply the wants of their own age, to respond to the demands of their own converts, they succeeded in producing writings that are timeless.

We hold, then, that it was in the good providence of God that the literary embodiment of the church's message came into being in a way that was wholly of God; *and* that, when the church was very young, it had no New Testament.

5

NO VOCABULARY OF ITS OWN

When the church was very young, it had no vocabulary of its own. All those terms that are now distinctive of Christianity had to be either borrowed or invented.

Springing as it did out of Judaism, the Christian movement possessed from the beginning a great deal that was easily described by Jewish terms. These terms were taken over bodily and belong to us as much as to the Old Testament believers.

The fact that the Old Testament had been translated into Greek, and that the Greek version was in common use wherever Greek-speaking Jews were to be found, meant that the Christian church had at its fingers a great collection of religious words, and that these words possessed a significance already fixed by Jewish scriptures. In this fact we see the world providentially prepared for Christianity. How great was the advantage of the early preachers in possessing a religious vocabulary of wide range and expression.

But Christianity was not a mere sect of Judaism. Time soon showed that it was not. Here was a new thing in the world, and it brought new ideas and new experiences which called for new forms of expression. Accordingly, along with words that had already been employed in the same sense in the Old Testament, *we find in the New Testament, fresh descriptions put with its new ideas.*

The most conspicuous illustration is the word by which the followers of Christ were called. Christ Himself was commonly referred to by the early preachers as "Jesus of Nazareth" (Acts 2:22; 3:6; 6:14; 22:8; 26:9) or "Jesus Christ of Nazareth" (4:10). As applied to the followers of Christ, the word "Nazarenes" is to be connected with the town to which Jesus belonged. In stating the charge against Paul at the court of the governor Felix, Tertullus described him as "a ringleader of the sect of the Nazarenes" (24:5). Evidently this was the name by which the followers of Jesus of Nazareth were widely known. It is amazing that this is *not* the main term used to describe us!

Early on, the movement was also referred to as "The Way" (9:2)—a rich expression that did not survive in the centuries that followed. At Ephesus several years later the same expression is used. Jewish opponents were "speaking evil of the Way before the multitude" (19:9), and again Demetrius is found provoking "no small stir concerning the Way" (19:23).

Was this term used because the outstanding feature of the new movement was a mode of life rather than a type of creed? The word "Way" certainly seems to fit in with the idea that we moderns express by "a new way of life."

We find other passages in which the word "Life" takes on a fuller significance. Jesus is "the Prince (or Author, or Captain) of Life, whom God raised from the dead" (3:15). The apostles, liberated from prison, are charged by the angel to "stand and speak in the temple to the people all the words of *this* Life" (5:20). The Jerusalem Christians, on hearing Peter's story of his visit to Cornelius, exclaim: "Then to the Gentiles also hath God granted repentance unto *life*" (11:18).

The word in its simplicity is even more striking than in the more familiar expression "eternal life."

A few further examples may be given which show that the church, when very young, was feeling round for the appropriate word by which to describe itself and its people!

An interesting case in point is *"apostle."* "Apostle" was employed by Jesus to describe the twelve whom He *specially* selected from the company of disciples (Luke 6:13), and to them it is almost exclusively applied in the New Testament. *But not quite!* Paul, at any rate, leaves no doubt of his claim to be regarded as an apostle equally with the rest (I Cor. 9:1). Luke also refers to Barnabas as well by the term "the apostles" (Acts 14:4,14). In writing to the Thessalonians, Paul brackets Silvanus and Timothy with himself as "apostles" (I Thes. 2:6).

So we see a word here that was being extended so as *to include an increasing number of the leading workers* in the church. Something arrested this tendency. In practice, this term has dropped out of use from the first century onwards.

The word *"disciple"* also has an interesting history. It was first applied to those who were in close personal touch with Jesus, as in pupils to Rabbi. It was continued in Acts as the regular description of those who became members of the Christian community. Then the word suddenly disappears. Nowhere else in the New Testament do we find it. Apparently it was recognized as being specially applicable to those who were attached to Christ as personal followers during His lifetime, and its use was restricted to that meaning.

Probably that is the meaning of the expression "an early disciple," used in referring to Mnason of Cyprus (Acts 21:16). He had been one of the original company. What might have happened to the word is hinted at in the story of Paul's escape from Damascus, where Luke says that *"his* disciples took him by night, and let him down through the wall" (9:25).

But the word as it was used here seems to have been stillborn. Nowhere else do we read of the word "disciples" except as referring to the Lord Jesus and his followers. Perhaps they remembered that he had said, "Be not ye called Rabbi, for one is your teacher, and all ye are brethren" (Matt. 23:8).

A church which had no fixed and rigid vocabulary, but which worked out its own terminology as it went along, selecting, modifying and rejecting, is an interesting phenomenon.

What do we see in this phenomenon? We see a church enjoying the liberty of the Spirit! She had the happy consciousness of being led in the various steps that she took. We, in turn, set all things in concrete. Such loyalty to the letter would indicate disloyalty to the Spirit.

The church that was once free to select and to decide such matters is still free to be liberated from forms, free from non-religious terms, and free to use new words to describe her experience to mankind. For the Spirit who led the first generation of Christ's followers is neither dead nor moribund, but available still in the fulness of His wisdom and His power to guide the affairs of Christ's church.

6

NO DOGMATIC SYSTEM

When the church was very young, she had no dogmas of her own, "no thought-out theology," [13] no exact and well-defined statement of Christian doctrine.

Every section of the Christian church today is prepared to give an account of its tenets. Doctrinal positions have been so fully worked out that every question one could raise has been provided with an astute answer. If one should think the last word has been spoken and the system perfect, the first step has been taken towards mental atrophy. *Our grasp of truth can never be final.* It must always be approximate, with the possibility of wider visions and clearer perceptions out there ahead somewhere.

13. Streeter, *The Primitive Church*, p. 45.

The early church had no elaborate statement of beliefs. Even the early creeds lay *centuries* ahead. All that the church had was a series of facts for its mind to work upon; and these facts were all connected with the life and ministry, the death and resurrection, of Jesus of Nazareth.

Let us look at the term "word" in this light. "They that were scattered abroad (after the death of Stephen) went about preaching the word" (8:4); but, nevertheless, "speaking the word to none save only to Jews" (11:19). While Peter was addressing Cornelius and his friends, "the Holy Ghost fell on all them which heard the word" (10:44). Paul and Barnabas spoke "the word in Perga" (14:25); but later on, Paul and Silas were "forbidden of the Holy Ghost to speak the word in Asia" (16:6). The Beroeans "received the word with all readiness of mind" (17:11); and in Corinth "Paul was constrained by the word" (18:5).

We cannot understand the expression in all these passages in the familiar modern sense of "the Bible" or" the New Testament." We have to recognize, with Luther, [14] the difference between "the word" and the printed book. The *word* is the Christian message, revealed,

14. *Encyclopaedia of Religion and Ethics*, viii, 203b.

reflected upon, presented and proclaimed. The *word* is the recognized statement of the Christian position and appeal.

This message had to be prepared by the apostles as they went along. That is, these mighty men were not provided with a specific or memorized message given by Christ.

The distinctive Christian message to the world was not "canned." It emerged.

In his first address on the day of Pentecost, Peter referred to Jesus as "a man approved of God unto you by mighty works and wonders and signs, which God did by him in the midst of you" (2:22). Then, after proclaiming the Lord's resurrection from the dead, Peter announced the Lord Jesus' exaltation "at the right hand of God" (v. 33), and challenged his hearers to accept the statement that "God hath made Him both Lord and Christ, this Jesus whom ye crucified" (v. 36).

Other expressions not familiar to us today nonetheless meet us in the early chapters of Acts. Jesus is "God's Servant" (3:13,26; 4:27,30), with a manifest reference to the Suffering Servant of Isa. 53. He is "the Holy and Righteous One" (3:14), "the Prince of Life" (3:15), "the Christ who hath been appointed for you" (3:20). "He is the stone which was set at naught of you the builders, which was made the head of the corner" (4:11). He is "a Prince and a Saviour," exalted by God to "give repentance to Israel and remission of sins" (5:31). Anointed by God with the Holy Ghost and with power, He "went about doing good, and healing all that were oppressed of the devil; for God was with Him" (10:38). Now "He is Lord of all" (10:36), and He is "ordained of God to be the Judge of quick and dead" (10:42).

These passages give some indication of the process that was going on in the hearts of the apostles while the church was very young. The Old Testament scriptures furnished them with terms that helped them convey the message of Jesus. In this connection we must remember that the Master Himself had been their guide (Chapter IV: p. 50f.). At the same time their words were often of the nature of a personal testimony.

When the church was very young, it had no written New Testament. Nonetheless, it was a true church, and it did the essential work that a church is raised up to do. She won converts and trained them to live useful lives and to spend themselves in the cause of Christ.

She kept her unity, a thing which became *impossible* later on when the philosophic Greek gained the upper hand in church councils.

To define is only too often to divide.

The attempt to define the Person of Christ beyond what was necessary for worship and for the mission of the church brought about divisions which have not yet been healed. Are we to turn the blessing passed on to us into a curse by elevating intellectual distinction into a position so important that Christians who cannot think alike must dwell in separate communities? And have no fellowship one with another? Not even meeting at the Lord's table? Better the simplicity, the immaturity and the inadequacy of the early church's simple teaching than such a contradiction of the spirit of Christ!

We come back to this: when the church was very young, "the theory of theology" formed no part of its message. The experience that came to men who accepted the offer of salvation was valid. And to all who will come to God through Christ, believing that God *is* what we see in Jesus, that same experience is available today ... without applying any theory of theology. Salvation does not come through a well-thought-out theology, but by venturing upon the God who has been revealed in Jesus Christ.

7

NO SABBATH REST

This chapter does *not* apply to the church at Jerusalem in the earliest days, but it does to the church in Gentile cities. In such cities, when the church was very young, it had no Sabbath.

Let us try to realize what this means. To the ordinary Christian born and brought up in a Christian land, one of the earliest experiences associated in his mind with religion is the observance of one special, religious day—a day marked by the closing of shops and the cessation of work, by attendance at religious services and by conduct unlike that of other days.

Religion and Sunday are by habit of mind inextricably connected. To break away from a particular method of observing Sunday is commonly regarded as the outward and visible sign of "back-sliding." It is hard for many of us to think of people being really religious and yet failing to observe Sunday in the conventional way. But if we wish to obtain an accurate idea of the life of the early church in a Gentile city, we must make that mental adjustment!

The seven-day division of time was known and observed in Greek and Roman society at the time of the Christian era. (The practice had come to Rome from Babylon via Egypt.) But not one of these seven days was special. Not one of the seven was religious, nor was any one of these seven days set aside for rest.

The holidays of the Romans did not come by days of the week. Holidays came by days of the month. You had a day to rest only at irregular intervals, on a day of some heathen festival.

Jewish settlers, on the other hand, maintained their sabbath customs even in a strange land. Their weekly day of rest and worship was widely known by others as one of their peculiarities. The sabbath day at the synagogue provided the apostles with one of their best opportunities for giving their message to the Jews (Acts 13:14, 42, 44; 17:2; 18:4; 16:13).

The apostles availed themselves of the opportunity but they did not include the observance of the sabbath as part of *their* message to the *Gentiles.* After Paul left the churches of Galatia and they began to observe "days and months and seasons and years," he treated this conduct as a sign of serious spiritual decline. "How turn ye back again to the weak and beggarly rudiments, whereunto ye desire to be in bondage over again?" (Gal. 4:9f.).

On the other hand, the division of a week into seven days was accepted as the status quo by all (I Cor. 16:2). Too, special significance of the *first* day is evident (Acts 20:7). The first day was the day of the Sun, but the Christians shrank from calling it by a name possessing heathen associations, so they called it *the Lord's day* (Rev. 1:10).

But *neither* by the Christians nor by their heathen neighbors was the first day of the week observed as a holiday, nor as a day of not working. The world's business went forward on that day, just as on other days. Any holidays or rest days came as a result of the erratic heathen celebrations. On the first day of the week they worked, *and* turned from their busy occupations to break bread and to pray.

Nor did they regard it as part of their message to advocate a weekly day of rest. Desirable as this might be from a humanitarian point of view, they had more important tasks to fulfill. The Christian church was most active and most expansive at a time when it had no "Sunday" as understood in the modern sense. The church made *no effort* to persuade the world to recognize a special day of rest.

"To suggest that the effectiveness of the Christian church stands or falls with the observance of the Lord's Day is to ignore or to misunderstand the precedent of the first three Christian centuries." [15]

From A.D. 321 onwards, the position was altered. After his conversion, Constantine decreed a general cessation of labor in the towns "on the venerable day of the Sun," exempting rural occupations since they were governed by the weather and the seasons.

We in the evangelical churches are the heirs of two distinct streams of tradition. One emphasizes sabbath observance and the other discredits it. First comes the Puritan inheritance, with its rigid sabbath-keeping. Unlike the early

15. *Preachers' Magazine*, April 1932, p. 143.

Reformers, the English Puritans identified the Lord's Day with the Sabbath (but observed one day after Saturday). They attempted to make everyone observe the sabbath rest as a part of the Christian religion.

In 1595 Nicholas Bownd, in a book entitled *The True Doctrine of the Sabbath*, boldly transferred to Sunday the whole observance of the Jewish Sabbath. He demanded this day of rest be enforced by law. Over a hundred books advocating such an attitude were published during the next century. [16] This extreme position gradually gave way as the Puritan movement came to an end.

The second tradition is far more recent. Indeed it has scarcely lasted long enough to be called a tradition. It arose from the modern concentration of interest in the life and teaching of Christ.

Virtually every reference to the Sabbath in connection with Christ implies a criticism of the whole contemporary view of that day. One of the counts *against* Jesus was that He was a Sabbath breaker. You don't get a reputation like that from a Puritan-like observance of the Sabbath! Jesus

16. *Expository Times*, July 1931, p. 440a.

exalted the inward and spiritual, and discounted the outward and formal. It is difficult, then, to attach importance to one day as holy above the rest. Those who have been brought up in this atmosphere cannot understand Christianity being identified or bound up with "sabbatarianism."

So far as the humanitarian aspect of the day is concerned, the preservation of Sunday as a day of rest must be left with those who wish to keep it that way, or to end it! But when it comes to the religious aspect of the day, the Christian can no longer invoke the aid of the law, or use any form of compulsion. Unless the day is consecrated to God in the spirit of glad willingness, it becomes a mere outward observance, of the kind that Jesus condemned. The expression "sabbath desecration" has no place in the Christian list of sins. It belongs to the Jewish list, which has been so thoroughly altered by the cross of Christ as to render much of it obsolete.

We find ourselves living in a world that goes about its pleasures and its recreations on Sunday, while a few people observe that day as the Lord's Day. The early church found itself in a world like that! The world pursued its ordinary occupations every day of the week, *including* the day that

Christians claimed for the Lord. There is a good deal of similarity between the two situations. We have this: the noise of the world's work is almost stilled; but the day's leisure is secular in nature. We, in turn can use the day for spiritual profit if we so desire.

In circumstances somewhat like our own, did the early church initiate a campaign for the observance of the Lord's Day? Obviously not. It would have been an impossible task, and it would have been beginning at the wrong end. Did the church then resign itself to an attitude of feeble impotence, confessing that it could do nothing without a special day to proclaim the gospel? By no means. If the church could not persuade people to attend Christian services on the day of the Sun, then the church had other ways ... contact with the unbeliever *every* day, while engaged in the ordinary course of the world's work. The church used all opportunities to influence their fellows for Christ.

We shall do well to realize the situation as it exists today.

For better and for worse, the general attitude towards Sunday has radically changed. Today there is far less opportunity of winning outsiders for Christ through our public services on the Lord's Day. That means that more constant and systematic use must be made of the opportunities provided in the common walks of *daily life*. The modern Christian, like his brothers and sisters of the early days, must witness his faith among neighbors, relatives and fellow workers. That was how the movement spread when the church was very young, when it had no sabbath, and no consecrated building, and only an occasional visit from a Christian worker as he passed through the region.

PART II

But it Did Possess:

An Experience

A Store of Teaching from Christ

A Gospel

8

AN EXPERIENCE

We come now to the things which the early church *did* possess. When it was very young, the church had an experience. We place that first above all else.

The Primitive Church had no New Testament, no thought-out theology, no stereotyped traditions. The men who took Christ to the Gentile world had received no formal or professional training, only a great experience. It was an experience in which "all maxims and philosophies were reduced to the simple task of walking in the light." [17]

Our task now is to explore the content and

17. *The Primitive Church*, p. 45f.

61

meaning of this experience which impelled them so incredibly.

Our thoughts turn first to the day of Pentecost. "There is to be found the secret we would discover, most of us would say. But is that true? No evangelical Christian is likely to underestimate the place of Pentecost in the life of the early church. A great experience indeed came to the church and the apostles on that day. It was to be an experience which would continue to influence the church all through the days that followed. The gift bestowed on that occasion came directly from their exalted Lord (Acts 2:33). That experience gave to the disciples the needed assurance that He still lived, that He was still concerned with the progress of His church.

There are, nonetheless, features in the story of Pentecost that seem to put it outside the realm of experiences that are likely to happen to us. The sound that came from heaven as of the rushing of a mighty wind; the tongues parting asunder like as of fire; the experience of speaking with other tongues as the Spirit gave them utterance—these suggest an element of uniqueness in the event. If the story of the apostolic experience is to have value for us, then what happened to them must be reproducible in our lives.

Now when we look into the matter, we find that what these men witnessed to was not Pentecost. These men witnessed to something which happened before Pentecost. Their own great experience began with Jesus Christ rather than with the Holy Spirit.

Let us try to analyze the experience that constituted the first great possession of these men. What was their obsession?

(1) We must begin with their three years' companionship with Jesus. "He appointed twelve, that they might be with Him" (Mark 3:14). That, in itself, was an experience of inestimable value.

To be with Jesus, in the sacred intercourse of those months and years—what other twelve men in the whole history of mankind ever enjoyed such a privilege! With Him through months of success and popularity, with Him through seasons of gloom and apparent failure; with Him in city and village, in the country and by the seashore, on mountain and lake; with Him while He was teaching and working miracles, while He was meeting the arguments of hostile Pharisees, and while He was taking little children in His arms; with Him in the crowds, and afterwards in the silence and the solitude; and all the time the wealth of His soul was being outpoured into their lives.

While He was on earth the energies of those three years were largely devoted to these men!

He seems to have regarded His private talks with His disciples as being equal in importance to all that He said publicly. When the crowds had dispersed, they could sit down with Him and ask Him quietly for further enlightenment. He encouraged them to ask questions, and many a valued passage in the gospels consists of the answers He gave them.

This was the experience which impelled these men. Not the teachings. Not the information. It was who He was! This changed them. From Him they came to understand what true spirituality was—this revising and superseding their ideas of goodness and piety. This was the first great element in their experience.

Jesus Himself had made the experience of their being with Him the chief point in their qualification for service.

"Ye also bear witness, because ye have been with me from the beginning" (John 15:27).

When a vacancy in their ranks arose through the death of Judas, what did they look for in a man as the supreme qualification for joining these ranks? It was that a man must have been with the Lord Jesus *from the beginning* (Acts 1:21).

(2) As time went on, the apostles became increasingly conscious of this being a qualification for all workers: a sense of the constant presence (and direction and help) of the risen, exalted and indwelling Christ. An unseen, but real and unmistakable Lord inside! The Master was fulfilling His promise to be with them all the days of their lives. (Matt. 28:20 mg.)

The indwelling presence of the Lord Jesus became the "replacement" of their companionship with Him in Galilee and Judea. It was expedient that He should go away in the *flesh* in order that He might be near to all His followers in the *spirit* (John 16:7). This was *their* privilege. But it is also an abiding privilege! It is an experience for all of us. It is possible for you and for me, as much to us as to the *first* generation! One man who did not know Christ after the flesh, as the original apostles had known Him, was nevertheless able to say, "I have been crucified with Christ; and it is no longer I who live, but Christ liveth in me" (Gal. 2:20 mg.). That man knew and experienced an indwelling Lord. He made it his chief concern to "know Him, and the power of His resurrection, and the fellowship of His sufferings" (Phil. 3:10). Paul had arrived at a sense of communion with Christ of the deepest and most intimate kind. It is a fellowship far closer than that of mere physical nearness. Far closer!

You and I may perhaps envy the apostles their privilege of companionship with Jesus. But we are not really handicapped here. If we cannot start quite where they started, we can fully share the experience they had with Christ after His ascension. It was a riper and more abiding experience, an experience of vital and intimate fellowship between each of them and a triumphant, ascended Lord.

(3) This abiding presence of Christ gave them a sense of power, of adequacy, of readiness to cope with any situation that arose.

These men were never at a loss to know the thing to do. Infinite resources of grace and wisdom and strength were available for them to draw upon—a reservoir in the unseen realms that could never be exhausted. Men who felt that all the resources possessed and exercised by Jesus in the days of His flesh were still waiting to be appropriated and used (John 14:12) would not shrink from any task that challenged them. Neither should we, if we had a like simple faith and confident trust and an experience with a living, reigning, indwelling Lord!

(4) These first Christian workers had an abounding joy, and a feeling that they *must* share with one another *and* with others this incredible thing that had happened to them and that had been entrusted to them.

Ten days before Pentecost, Luke describes these men as returning to Jerusalem with great joy, continually blessing God in the temple (24:52 f.). After Pentecost, the description is repeated: "They did take their food with gladness and singleness of heart, praising God, and having favour with all the people" (Acts 2:46 f.). Towards others, they displayed an intense desire to impart their "good tidings," and any other boon it was in their power to bestow.

(5) The conviction crystallized in them that this good thing which they possessed was what the world needed, and it really was their task to tell the world about it.

"Here in Christ, and only in Christ, is salvation," says Peter. In that conviction they went out into the world and offered Christ as the only adequate Savior. This dynamic drive had its wellsprings in a fellowship with an indwelling Lord.

As John puts it, in his quiet, impressive way: "That which was from the beginning, that which we have seen with our eyes, that which we beheld, and our hands handled, concerning the Word of life ... that which we have seen and heard declare we unto you, that ye also may have fellowship with us (I John 1:1,3).

Dare we say a great experience is not everything? Then hear an angel. "Go," said the angel, "and stand and speak in the temple to the people all the words of *this Life*" (5:20. See Chap. V, p. 64).

Life! Abundant life! eternal life! Life with a richness and savor and quality and power of communicating itself, such as had never before been experienced. The very life of God. If there is life, and the means of sustaining it, it does not much matter what else is missing. Life can propagate itself, can create its own forms and instruments. Life contains within itself the hope and the possibility and the promise of unending progress. In the early church, a great deal was missing which later centuries regarded as important! But we would all gladly give up these things if only we might have more life—a fuller, richer, deeper, more vital experience of the presence and power of the living Christ!

'Tis Life, of which our nerves are scant,
More life, and richer, that we want.

If the yearning for life is real and sincere, it will show itself by a resolve to begin where the apostles began! That yearning to know Him will show itself in a closer intimacy and a more constant fellowship with Christ. After all, *He* is the Way! *That* is because *He* is the life. The spiritual efficiency to meet those needs will be there when we are in the presence of His life. Men will take knowledge of us, as they did of the apostles, that we have been with Jesus (4:13).

9

A STORE OF TEACHING
FROM CHRIST

When the church was very young, it also had a store of teaching received from Christ. An "experience" might possibly be thought of as an emotional state, a transient sentiment. Had that been all the church had when it was young, it would quickly have subsided, the members in the movement left flat and spiritless. But Jesus had given to the disciples something so profound, we are thinking about it still, with a growing conviction that there is food for thought not only for their age and ours, but for all those yet to come.

The gospels were written down at a time when it could be checked by those who heard Him speak. What He did and what He said was committed to literary form while still fresh in the memories of the apostles. With *this* the apostles "filled Jerusalem."

Paul charges Timothy to "guard the deposit" (I Tim. 6:20), and that deposit of truth had come first from Christ Himself. From the earliest days, the disciples had "continued stedfastly in the apostles' teaching" (Acts 2:42). The body of truth as proclaimed by Jesus in the hearing of the apostles was one of the distinctive things that held them together in fellowship.

The early church, then, had not only an experience, but also teachings from the lips of Jesus. His teachings, which he handed down to His disciples, were, of course, the result of *His* own experience.

What constituted "the deposit" which Timothy was exhorted to guard? Jesus brought to mankind a new revelation of God, based on "being there." All other previously held concepts of God *and* our relationship to Him paled.

To our own generation the teaching of Jesus presents a challenge from which there is no escaping. Whenever we aim at something higher than our present attainment, whenever we reach out for something better, it is always in terms of Christ.

Is not this, then, the true wealth of the church? Is not the church abundantly enriched if it possesses this treasure of Christ's words coming forth from out of who He was and what *He* experienced. The early church, poor in other respects, was rich in its possession. Her aim was to broadcast the message that the stored-up memories of the original hearers had drawn upon. For the present-day church, here is the heritage that is best worth holding and the best worth distributing. The teaching of Jesus, coming out of His spiritual storehouse, is the *word* of life for a new *way* of life. Unless the hope for a better world is to remain for ever unrealized, we must preserve for ourselves and proclaim to mankind the words of our Lord Jesus. There is no other message that will meet the world's need.

10

A GOSPEL

When the church was very young, it had a gospel. The experience of the church was one the church knew it *had* to share. The church simply could do no other.

"We cannot but speak the things which we saw and heard" (Acts 4:20).

The church's store of teaching and experience was of such importance that the urge to spread it was irresistible. "Ye have filled Jerusalem with your teaching" (5:28).

Where many religious systems have failed is in their inability to provide the dynamic which will set men free from sin and the bondage of evil. Man needs help from outside himself to counteract the inherent downward pull.

The message of the New Testament has a ring of gladness in its delivery.

"The great delight which Jesus certainly intended and expected to give to all who received Him, His joy in giving and theirs in receiving, is a joy that has passed beyond our ability to conceive." [18] The apostles in the early days shared with men this joyful spirit of the Master.

The message announced proved to be a veritable message of glad tidings.

This new spiritual discovery the apostles continued to test, ever further and further afield. Would it work under other conditions than those at Jerusalem and among people of a different religious background? They "tried it out." The sphere of operation widened out to Damascus, Phoenicia, Cyprus, Antioch, Asia Minor; thence into Europe, to such cities as Philippi, Thessalonica, Corinth, and at last to Rome. In all sorts of communities, Jews, Gentiles, citizens and slaves, learned and ignorant, the effect of the message was tested. The result? "The word of God, *which also worketh* in you that believe" (I Thess. 2:13).

18. Lily Dougall, *Pro Christo et Ecclesia*, pp. 149, 151.

It works! Paul, having preached the word in the cities of Galatia and elsewhere, brought it over to the western side of the Aegean and wondered whether, under different conditions, similar results would follow. With a sense of deep joy and satisfaction he told his converts how he "thanked God without ceasing" for the way in which they had "received the word of the message." The experience confirmed that the gospel of the grace of God in Christ is the very thing that the world most deeply needed.

A gospel that will *work* is the finest possession that men can have. The apostles had such a gospel. We *still* have it: and it *still* works!

The world of that day was dissatisfied with the old pagan religion and was eagerly looking for something truer and more satisfying. A waiting world gave to the early church its opportunity to go ahead and present its message.

Today there is reason to believe that men cannot and will not be permanently satisfied without a living experience of Christ and His church as the foundation of their life. We have the message that will awaken the sense of need among our fellowmen and will at the same time afford the most complete satisfaction. A great responsibility rests upon us.

There is danger, then, getting off on side-lines. The world cannot be expected to think much of our gospel or a desire to have it, if *we* manifest so little confidence in it as to sell *accessories* along with our main product. The gospel of the grace of God is the stock-in-trade of the church. Not sold for money, it is offered freely as the gift of God in Christ. We have no other business, so we have no businesss adding to that gospel.

When the church was young, met in homes and lived in a world of its own unique community, it had a simple primitive gospel; and that gospel worked. Richer than the early church in many things, let us not forfeit all our advantage by accepting poverty in the main thing. They were experienced in many things of which we are ignorant, ignorant in so much of what we have. Let us get back to first things. Whatever else they could or could not offer to men, the church when young could offer a Savior, and then offer *the church* as a place for those who were saved to live out their lives!

When the church was very young, it had a gospel; and now that the church is no longer young, but tempted to think of itself as entitled to the reliefs and relaxations of advancing years, the church has nothing better than the gospel to give to the world.

PUBLISHER'S POST SCRIPT

In reading Rev. Loosley's book we were struck with one thing that was more or less left out. When the church was young, she had one other thing to give. And no other movement or religion had ever given anything even remotely similar to this.

What was this new and wondrous element of the church when young? She had *herself* to give. When a man met Christ—when the church was young—he was awed at the riches he received in having an indwelling Lord. *Then* he came into *the community of believers* and was awed again. The wonder of the daily fellowship, the care, the protection and "community" of the church . . . brand new creation . . . was a totally new experience for mankind. Saved men were a different species and they had a *habitat* to live in that was unique to that species. No one had ever known anything like the church . . . the community of the redeemed. Here was the *other* great magnetism of the church when she was young. Herself!

Today the Church is *not* young, and the one thing she so rarely gives is the indescribable, unattainable joy of living inside her invisible walls in the fellowship of Christ, in the midst of other brothers and sisters. It is high time she rediscovered the glory of herself, her beauty, her magnetism. A world looked on the community of the believer in ancient times and was utterly befuddled, mystified, awed—and a little bit curious—about the believers' way of living so knit together with others, their joy at always being together, and their total fraternity in their daily living. *This* was her greatest attraction to onlookers. It is high time she began to get back this divine element which makes her so beautiful and draws men spellbound to her . . . and thence to her Lord.

BOOKS by Gene Edwards

DIVINE ROMANCE

"How can I go about loving the Lord personally, intimately?" No book ever written will help more in answering this question for you. Not quite allegory, not quite parable, here is the most beautiful story on the love of God you have ever read. Beginning in eternity past, you will see your Lord unfold the only purpose for which He created all things. Plunging into time and space, you behold a breathtaking saga as He pursues His purpose, to have a bride! See His love story through His eyes. Be present at the crucifixion and resurrection as viewed from the heavenly realms. You will read the most glorious and powerful rendition of the crucifixion and resurrection ever described. The story reaches its climax at the end of the ages in a heart-stopping scene of the Lord at last taking His bride unto Himself. When you have finished this book, you will know the centrality of His love for you. A book that can set a flame in your heart to pour out your love upon Him.

A TALE OF THREE KINGS

A book beloved around the world. A dramatically told tale of Saul, David and

Absalom, on the subject of brokenness. A book used in the healing of the lives of many Christians who have been devastated by church splits and by injuries suffered at the hands of other Christians.

OUR MISSION

A group of Christian young men in their early twenties met together for a weekend retreat to hear Gene Edwards speak. Unknown to them, they were about to pass through a catastrophic split. These messages were delivered to prepare those young men spiritually for the inevitable disaster facing them. Edwards presents the standard of the first century believers and how those believers walked when passing through similar crises. A remarkable statement on how a Christian is to conduct himself in times of strife, division and crisis. A book every Christian, every minister, every worker will need at one time or another in his life.

THE INWARD JOURNEY

A study in transformation, taking the reader through a journey from time's end to grasp the ways of God in suffering and the cross, and to bring an understanding to why He works the way He does.

LETTERS TO A DEVASTATED CHRISTIAN

Edwards writes a series of letters to a Christian devastated by the authoritarian movement, who has found himself on the edge of bitterness.

PREVENTING A CHURCH SPLIT

This is a study in the anatomy of church splits, what causes them, their root causes, the results, and how to prevent them. A book every Christian will need someday. This book could save your spiritual life, and perhaps that of your fellowship.

CHURCH HISTORY:
These two books bring to bear a whole new perspective on church life.

REVOLUTION, THE STORY OF THE EARLY CHURCH, Vol. 1
This book tells, in a "you are there" approach, what it was like to be a Christian in the first century church, recounting the events from Pentecost to Antioch. By Gene Edwards.

THE TORCH OF THE TESTIMONY
John W. Kennedy tells the little known, almost forgotten, story of evangelical Christians during the dark ages.

BOOKS By Jeanne Guyon

EXPERIENCING THE DEPTHS OF JESUS CHRIST

Guyon's first and best known book. One of the most influential pieces of Christian literature ever penned on the deeper Christian life. Among the multitudes of people who have read this book and urged others to read it are: John Wesley, Adoniram Judson, Watchman Nee, Jesse Penn-Lewis, Zinzendorf, and the Quakers. A timeless piece of literature that has been on the "must read" list of Christians for 300 years.

FINAL STEPS IN CHRISTIAN MATURITY

This book could well be called volume two of **Experiencing The Depths of Jesus Christ.** Here is a look at the experiences a more advanced and faithful Christian might encounter in his/her walk with the Lord. Without question, next to **Experiencing The Depths,** here is Mme. Jeanne Guyon's best book.

UNION WITH GOD

Written as a companion book to Experiencing The Depths of Jesus Christ, and includes 22 of her poems.

GENESIS
SONG OF SONGS

Jeanne Guyon wrote a commentary on the Bible; here are two of those books. *SONG OF SONGS* has been popular through the centuries and has greatly influenced several other well-known commentaries on the Song of Songs.

THE SPIRITUAL LETTERS OF MADAME GUYON

Here is spiritual counseling at its very best. There is a Christ-centeredness to Jeanne Guyon's counsel that is rarely, if ever, seen in Christian literature.

THE WAY OUT

A spiritual study of Exodus as seen from "the interior way."

THE BOOK OF JOB

Guyon looks at the life of Job from the view of the deeper Christian life.

CHRIST OUR REVELATION

A profound and spiritual look at the book of Revelation.

OTHER BOOKS BY CHRISTIAN BOOKS

TURKEYS AND EAGLES, by Peter Lord

Hagen and Selin have been abandoned by their parents. But they have been adopted by a flock of turkeys. Are they eagles? Or are they turkeys? Or is it possible they are eagles that have been turkeyized? But even more important, is it possible that the greatest of all tragedies has befallen you? Are you an eagle that has been turkeyized, an eagle that doesn't even know he is an eagle?

This book could very well transform your life, for it has profoundly affected the thousands of Christians who have heard Peter Lord tell the story.

In the finest tradition of Christian story telling, which dates back all the way to the Lord's parables, this masterfully told tale contains the very heart of the gospel as it pertains to living the Christian life.

AUTOBIOGRAPHY OF JESUS CHRIST

Matthew, Mark, Luke and John are blended together into one complete story of the life of Jesus Christ told in the first person. It is as though you are reading the diary of the Lord Jesus Christ.

A unique and wonderful devotional tool and a totally new discovery of the greatest story ever told, the greatest life ever lived.

(Conferences on the deeper Christian Life are held annually through the United States. Write for further information.)

89

The following prices are for the year 1988 only; please write for our catalog for price updates and for new releases. All books are paperback unless otherwise noted.

Turkeys & Eagles (Peter Lord)	$ 9.95
Autobiography of Jesus Christ (hb)	$ 9.95
on cassette tape (6 tape set in album)	$29.95
Preventing a Church Split (Edwards) (hb)	$ 9.95
A Tale of Three Kings (Edwards)......................	$ 6.95
The Divine Romance (Edwards) ($10.95 hb)	$ 7.95
Experiencing the Depths of Jesus Christ (Guyon).........	$ 6.95
The Inward Journey (Edwards)	$ 7.95
Letters to a Devastated Christian (Edwards)	$ 4.95
Our Mission (Edwards)	$ 7.95
Revolution, Vol. 1 (Edwards)	$ 6.95
Practicing His Presence (Lawrence, Laubach)	$ 6.95
Union with God (Guyon)	$ 6.95
Final Steps in Christian Maturity (Guyon)	$ 6.95
The Spiritual Guide (Molinos)........................	$ 6.95
Torch of the Testimony (Kennedy).....................	$ 7.95
Mme. Guyon's Letters	$ 6.95
Fenelon's Letters...................................	$ 6.95
Guyon's Commentaries:	
Genesis	$ 6.95
Exodus (The Way Out)............................	$ 6.95
Song of Songs	$ 6.95
Job...	$ 7.95
Revelation (Christ, Our Revelation)	$ 7.95
The Passing of the Torch (Chen)	$ 6.95
When the Church Was Young (Loosley)...............	$ 7.95

Christian Books Publishing House
The Seedsowers
P.O. Box 3368
Auburn, Maine 04210
207-783-4234
Visa-MasterCard accepted
These books are available through your local Christian book store.